El Dorado County Library

Donated by
A Generous
South Lake Tahoe
Patron

MISSION: NUTRITION

Food Options: Following Special Diets

KRISTIN PETRIE MS, RD

ABDO Publishing Company

visit us at
www.abdopublishing.com

Published by ABDO Publishing Company, 8000 West 78th Street, Edina, Minnesota 55439.
Copyright © 2012 by Abdo Consulting Group, Inc. International copyrights reserved in all
countries. No part of this book may be reproduced in any form without written permission from the
publisher. The Checkerboard Library™ is a trademark and logo of ABDO Publishing Company.

Printed in the United States of America, North Mankato, Minnesota.
062011
092011

 PRINTED ON RECYCLED PAPER

Cover Photos: Glow Images, iStockphoto
Interior Photos: AP Images pp. 7, 12; Corbis pp. 5, 12, 22–23; Getty Images pp. 8, 11, 17, 20–21,
    27, 29; Glow Images pp. 9, 15, 18–19; iStockphoto pp. 1, 25

Series Coordinator: BreAnn Rumsch
Editors: Megan M. Gunderson, BreAnn Rumsch
Art Direction: Neil Klinepier

Library of Congress Cataloging-in-Publication Data

Petrie, Kristin, 1970-
 Food options : following special diets / Kristin Petrie.
    p. cm. -- (Mission: Nutrition)
 Includes index.
 ISBN 978-1-61783-084-6
 1. Nutrition--Juvenile literature 2. Food--Juvenile literature. I. Title.
 RA784.P478 2012
 613.2--dc22
                        2011011085

Contents

A Fitting Diet 4

Bad, Bad Fads 6

Diet for Health 10

Mediterranean Medicine 14

Vegetarian Vibe 16

Allergy Alert! 20

Eating Green 24

Fast-Food Fix 26

A Healthier You 28

Glossary 30

Web Sites 31

Index 32

A Fitting Diet

More than likely, you've heard of several kinds of diets. These may include the vegetarian and Mediterranean diets. Maybe you've also heard of the raw food, Zone, and Atkins diets. What are all these diets? And why do people follow them?

The word *diet* often makes people think of weight loss. But a diet is actually whatever a person eats on a regular basis. A healthy diet is based on eating moderate amounts of many kinds of foods. It meets the body's needs for growth, activity, and everyday functions.

People change their diets for many reasons. These include having medical conditions and wanting to look or feel better. Some special diets have many health benefits. Yet others can actually be harmful, especially for growing kids like you.

Therefore, kids should never change their diet without talking to a parent, doctor, or **nutrition** expert. This is especially important with so many special diet options to choose from! Keep reading to clear up the confusion.

Growing kids should always follow expert advice when eating a special diet.

Bad, Bad Fads

Look at any magazine rack, and you'll see covers blasting miracle diet claims. Some make promises such as, "Shed Five Pounds in Five Days!" Others say, "Improve Your Brainpower!"

Most of these diets are meant to bring about weight loss. Others promise to cleanse the body. To produce quick results, these fad diets usually cheat the body of important **nutrients**. And, those quick results rarely last long.

During the early 2000s, dieters went mad for meat! People following the Atkins diet ate foods high in **protein**, such as eggs and meat. And they cut out foods with **carbohydrates**. These included white bread, rice, fruits, and sugary treats.

Not everyone supports this type of diet. Reducing candy and other treats can be good for you. But cutting out fruits and other healthy foods is a bad idea. In fact, avoiding any food group is always a red flag for a fad.

Today, detox diets are popular. They promise to clean out your body. These diets require **fasting** or taking pills, powders, or herbs. This forces your body to get rid of lots of water and solid waste. It might seem like you are losing weight. Still, these diets probably do not clean out toxins like they promise. Your liver and kidneys already do that for you!

Fad diets are bad news for kids. Avoiding foods your body needs can slow your growth. You might end up shorter than if you had eaten a healthy diet! And, your body may not be able to fight off illness.

Fad diets are dangerous for another reason. They usually

It's okay to have the treats you want. Just be sure to eat them in moderation.

Boys, you may feel pressure to be strong and athletic. But remember, your body will develop at its own healthy rate. For now, eat well and stay active!

begin with the desire to look like someone else. This could be a thin model or a muscular actor. Advertisements may make us feel we need to look a certain way. The problem with this is that everyone's body is different!

A change in weight will not change your natural body shape, height, or build. Dieting to reach impossible goals may lead to a dangerous eating disorder.

Danger Decoder

An eating disorder is one of several serious medical conditions. People with anorexia eat little to no food. Those with bulimia may eat. But they will avoid digesting any food by using the bathroom right after meals. Other kids may exercise too much.

Do you, or someone you know, have these behaviors? If so, tell a parent or a teacher, counselor, coach, or doctor. There is no need to be embarrassed or scared. These adults will not judge or scold you. Rather, they will help you get back on track to a healthy you.

If you are unhappy with your weight, talk to an adult before starting a diet. A parent, doctor, or **nutrition** expert can help find a healthy diet that's right for you.

How do you feel about your body? Learning to appreciate how you look will help build your confidence.

Diet for Health

Sometimes, a young person needs to gain or lose weight for health reasons. Some kids need to gain weight after a long illness. Eating more will boost their **immunity** and fuel growth. Other kids need to shed extra weight. This helps lower the risk of **diabetes** and high blood pressure.

Are you trying to gain or lose weight? Either way, the **calories** you take in must be balanced! Slow, steady weight change is the goal. Doctors usually recommend a healthy, balanced diet and physical activity.

A special diet can also help manage a disease. For example, people who have diabetes must watch their **carbohydrates**.

Danger Decoder

Remember that all kids grow at their own normal rate. Some are bigger and some are smaller than others. If being too thin or too heavy concerns you, ask for help. Good advice from an expert will help you change your diet without causing harm. Growing bodies need balanced meals!

Replacing unhealthy fats with healthier options lowers the risk of heart disease.

They need to eat enough, but not too many. This helps keep their bodies running well.

During **digestion**, **carbohydrates** become glucose. Glucose travels in your blood and provides energy. Insulin helps it move from your blood to your body's cells. But with **diabetes**, this process doesn't happen as it should. A balanced diet and medicine help manage the problem.

Oftentimes, following a special diet can help people improve their heart health. The term *heart disease* is used for several heart problems. These include high blood pressure and heart attack.

Fat and **cholesterol** from food can collect in blood vessels. That leaves less room for blood to flow through them. And eating too much salt makes your body hold in extra water. This increases the pressure inside the blood vessels.

Heart-healthy diets limit unhealthy fats, cholesterol, and salt. However, this type of diet is not all about taking foods away. It often involves eating oranges, spinach, and other foods rich in potassium and calcium. They help reduce blood pressure. Nuts, seeds, and fish contain healthy fats. Eating them protects the heart and blood vessels from future damage.

But you're just a kid, and these are grown-up problems, right? Wrong! Today, more kids are developing health problems that used to affect only adults. Following a healthy diet now can help prevent these problems from starting.

Mediterranean Medicine

One popular heart-healthy diet you may have heard of is the Mediterranean diet. This diet is inspired by the foods eaten in the areas surrounding the Mediterranean Sea.

Researchers know that Mediterranean people eat a diet that is high in fat. Yet, they have a lower risk of heart disease than most Americans. How could a high-fat diet result in fewer heart attacks?

The difference lies in the types of fat eaten. As you know, healthy fats don't harm the heart. Mediterranean people take in large amounts of olive oil, fish, nuts, and seeds. All of these foods contain healthy fats.

Why should people who don't live near the Mediterranean eat this way? Following the Mediterranean diet keeps people healthy in lots of ways! It lowers the risk of heart disease, certain **cancers**, and **Alzheimer's disease**.

The Mediterranean lifestyle focuses on activity and relationships. Along with a healthy diet, this offers many health benefits.

Vegetarian Vibe

Today, more and more people are following a vegetarian diet. You may even have a friend or a classmate who eats this way. But what is this special diet?

Vegetarians do not eat meat, poultry, or fish. Instead, they eat mostly plant foods. They fill up on grains, nuts, seeds, **legumes**, fruits, and vegetables.

There are several types of vegetarians. Some still eat foods other than meat that come from animals. Lacto-vegetarians drink milk and eat yogurt and cheese. Lacto-ovo vegetarians also include eggs in their diet.

Someone following a vegan diet eats only plant foods. These total vegetarians avoid all meats, fish, and foods that come from animals. For example, they will not eat a chicken or the eggs it lays.

Being vegan is more than a diet. It is a lifestyle. Vegans do not use products made from animals, such as leather or wool. They are also careful to not buy products that companies tested on animals.

It's not hard to create healthy, tasty meals without meat!

Why do people follow vegetarian diets? Many choose them for health reasons. They are rich in fruits and vegetables. And they are low in unhealthy fats. Diets with these qualities lower the risk of many health conditions. These include **obesity**, heart disease, and certain **cancers**.

Other people follow vegetarian diets out of concern for animals. They oppose the way animals are raised for our food supply. So, they avoid animal-based foods out of respect for animals.

As with all diets, kids should not jump into a vegetarian diet without help. Some important **nutrients** are usually gained through eating animal products. So vegetarian kids must eat a wider variety of plant foods than most kids do.

With expert advice, a vegetarian kid can meet all his or her body's needs. A **nutrition** professional can help you determine if a vegetarian diet is right for you. Together, you can make sure the diet has a healthy variety of foods.

Some animal lovers believe it is cruel to raise animals for food.

Healthy Habits

Vegetarians need to be sure they get enough:
- protein   • iron   • zinc   • vitamin D   • vitamin B_{12} • calcium

Vegetables, beans, lentils, and grains all provide protein. Whole grains and leafy greens, such as spinach, are good sources of iron and zinc. Vitamins B_{12} and D are available in fortified foods such as breakfast cereals and soy milk. Milk, yogurt, and cottage cheese are good calcium sources for lacto-vegetarians.

Allergy Alert!

Chances are, you are not allowed to bring peanut butter and jelly sandwiches to school. Candy, granola bars, or other foods with peanuts are not allowed, either. You probably also know why this rule exists. Some kids at your school are allergic to peanuts.

But what does this mean? Does it really matter if your trail mix has a few peanuts in it? Maybe the treats you brought in were made on equipment that also makes stuff with peanuts. Would passing them around the

classroom hurt someone? The truth is, yes! These things may be a real danger to someone with a peanut allergy.

An allergic response happens when the body thinks a food is harmful. To protect itself, the body makes an army of **antibodies**. They try to battle the harmful food.

For some people, this response is mild. It may include a runny nose and itchy eyes. But for others, the response is severe. They may experience difficulty breathing or a drop in blood pressure. Left untreated, these serious reactions can lead to death.

Luckily, people with food allergies can avoid these dangers by following elimination diets. These diets usually involve avoiding all foods that contain the **allergen**. Eight types of foods account for 90% of allergic reactions. These are milk, eggs, peanuts, tree nuts, fish, shellfish, soy, and wheat.

Is your school lunch allergy friendly?

Be sensitive to your classmates or teammates by sharing allergy-friendly foods.

Removing foods from your diet can be very challenging. It should not be done without expert help. Your doctor can help you find out if you have a true allergy. Then, a **nutrition** expert can help you safely cut out foods you can't eat.

Following a special diet will help you feel better. You may find you have more energy. Your itchy eyes, runny nose, upset stomach, or other reactions will go away.

Again, why should food allergies matter to you? Well, they are becoming more common. You probably know someone who has one. And they are depending on you to help them stay well. Respect their needs, or you'll put them at risk. In severe cases, knowing and avoiding certain foods may save your life or someone else's.

Eating Green

Today, many consumers realize that what they eat affects the planet. Some of them are taking action by going green. But how does someone save the **environment** with what they eat?

First, cut back on eating red meat. Have you recently eaten a hamburger? The cow it came from passed lots of gas. And that contributed to **climate change**!

Eating foods as close as possible to their whole, or natural, state is also Earth friendly. For example, eat baked potatoes instead of French fries. Have an apple instead of apple juice. Whole foods require little to no processing. This saves energy and creates less waste.

Buying organic foods is another positive step for the planet and your health. These foods are grown without harmful chemicals. This keeps our soil and groundwater cleaner.

What's the next step? Locavores buy foods grown and made locally whenever possible. This means they avoid foods that are packaged and available out of season. If it's February in

On average, food travels 1,300 miles (2,100 km) from farm to table. Eating local helps limit this distance!

Wisconsin, they know those grocery store grapes came from far away.

Some local shoppers buy produce and meat from farmers markets and community supported agriculture, or a CSA. They like getting local products while supporting their community. Growing food in your own garden is another fun way to eat locally.

Fast-Food Fix

By now, you can probably see that special diets require attention and planning. But people today are busy! So they often eat on the run. A drive-through or pizza delivery is easy when there is no time to cook.

Unfortunately, these common fast fixes lack proper **nutrition**. They don't provide variety. Instead, they give you lots of salt and unhealthy fats. Fast food is okay to eat once in a while. But what can your family do to make better choices the rest of the time? Get creative!

A busy schedule can mean eating in the car. So pack a healthy snack instead of hitting the drive-through. This healthier option will get you through your activity. Then, you can have a balanced meal when you get home.

Back at home and still pushed for time? Get many food groups in one bite! Pizza loaded with vegetables does the job. Taco salad with lean beef is another easy meal that packs a punch.

There are many special diets to consider. The right one for you depends on your health, activities, and beliefs. But remember, starting a special diet requires help. A parent, doctor, or **nutrition** expert can make sure your special diet still helps you grow strong and healthy.

Dried fruit, nuts, and granola are all healthy, filling snacks. Even better, they can be stashed in your car, backpack, or sports bag!

A Healthier You

Have you, or someone you know, recently switched to a special diet? You now understand that balance is key to staying healthy. But how do you eat healthily when certain foods are off limits? Whether you avoid meat or wheat, these simple ideas from the *Let's Move!* program can help.

KNOW YOUR NUTRIENTS! Learn what foods can replace the health benefits of foods you can't eat. What if you can't drink milk? You can eat lots of broccoli for calcium instead! What if you don't eat meat? You can get protein from beans and nuts.

EAT COLOR! Fruits and veggies are packed with important nutrients that your body needs. The variety of these colorful foods is so large, there's something for everybody. And more plants means less meat, which is even better for you.

Let's Move!

For more information, check out *Let's Move!* online at **www.letsmove.gov**.

Let's Move! is a campaign started by First Lady Michelle Obama to raise a healthier generation of kids and combat childhood obesity. This movement works to provide schools, families, and communities with the tools to help kids be more active, eat better, and live healthfully.

The *Let's Move!* Web site provides information about the movement. It includes recipes as well as helpful tips on nutrition and physical activity. And, there are action tools to promote healthier foods in your local schools or start a *Let's Move!* Meetup.

SWITCH OUT SODA! Studies show that Americans get 7% of their calories from soft drinks. That is more than they get from vegetables. Yikes! Next time you feel thirsty, reach for a glass of water, juice, or milk instead. These beverages satisfy your thirst and provide nutrients.

Glossary

allergen - a substance that causes an allergy.

Alzheimer's disease - an illness that causes forgetfulness, confusion, and overall mental disintegration.

antibody - a substance produced by special cells of the body to fight an attack, such as by a disease or an allergen.

calorie - the unit of measure for the energy supplied by food.

cancer - any of a group of often deadly diseases marked by harmful changes in the normal growth of cells. Cancer can spread and destroy healthy tissues and organs.

carbohydrate (cahr-boh-HEYE-drayt) - a substance made by plants, which serves as a major class of foods for animals. Sugar and starch are examples of carbohydrates.

cholesterol - a waxy substance that is present in animal cells and tissues. It is important in bodily processes but may thicken or harden arteries when too much is present.

climate change - a long-term change in Earth's climate, or in that of a region on Earth. It includes changing temperatures, weather patterns, and more. It can result from natural processes or human activities.

diabetes - a disease in which the body cannot properly absorb normal amounts of sugar and starch.

digestion - the process of breaking down food into simpler substances the body can absorb.

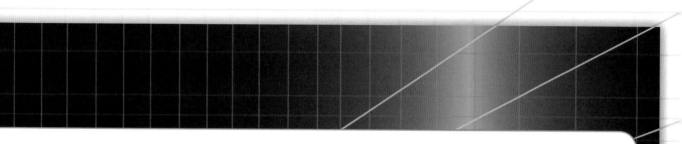

environment - all the surroundings that affect the growth and well-being of a living thing.

fast - to go without food.

immunity - the ability to resist a disease.

legume - a type of plant that bears pods, including peas, beans, and peanuts.

nutrient - a substance found in food and used in the body. It promotes growth, maintenance, and repair.

nutrition - that which promotes growth, provides energy, repairs body tissues, and maintains life.

obesity - the condition of having too much body fat.

protein - a substance which provides energy to the body and serves as a major class of foods for animals. Foods high in protein include cheese, eggs, fish, meat, and milk.

To learn more about following special diets, visit ABDO Publishing Company online. Web sites about food options are featured on our Book Links page. These links are routinely monitored and updated to provide the most current information available.

www.abdopublishing.com

Index

A
animal welfare 16, 18

B
body image 8, 9

C
cholesterol 13
climate change 24
community supported
    agriculture 25

D
dairy 16, 21, 26
dieting dangers 4, 6, 7, 8
diseases 10, 13, 14, 18

E
Earth-friendly diets 24, 25
eating disorders 8
eggs 6, 16, 21
elimination diets 21, 23

F
fad diets 4, 6, 7, 8
farmers markets 25
fast-food diets 26
fish 13, 14, 16, 21
food allergies 20, 21, 23
fruits 6, 13, 16, 18, 24, 25

G
gardening 25
grains 6, 16, 20, 26
growth 4, 7, 10, 27

H
health benefits 4, 6, 10,
    13, 14, 18, 23, 27
healthy fats 13, 14
heart-healthy diets 13,
    14

I
insulin 13

L
locavores 24, 25

M
meat 6, 16, 24, 25, 26
Mediterranean diet 4,
    14

N
nutrition expert 4, 9,
    18, 23, 27
nuts 13, 14, 16, 21

O
obesity 18
oil 14
organic foods 24

P
peanuts 20, 21

S
salt 13, 26
seeds 13, 14, 16
soy 21
sugar 6, 20

U
unhealthy fats 13, 18, 26

V
vegan lifestyle 16
vegetables 13, 16, 18,
    24, 25, 26
vegetarian diets 4, 16,
    18

W
weight 4, 6, 7, 8, 9, 10
wheat 21
whole foods 24